Would You Rather Have **TEETH** like a **T-REX** or **ARMOUR** like an **ANKYLOSAURUS?**

Camilla de la Bédoyère and Mel Howells

Would you rather...

have teeth like
a T- rex,

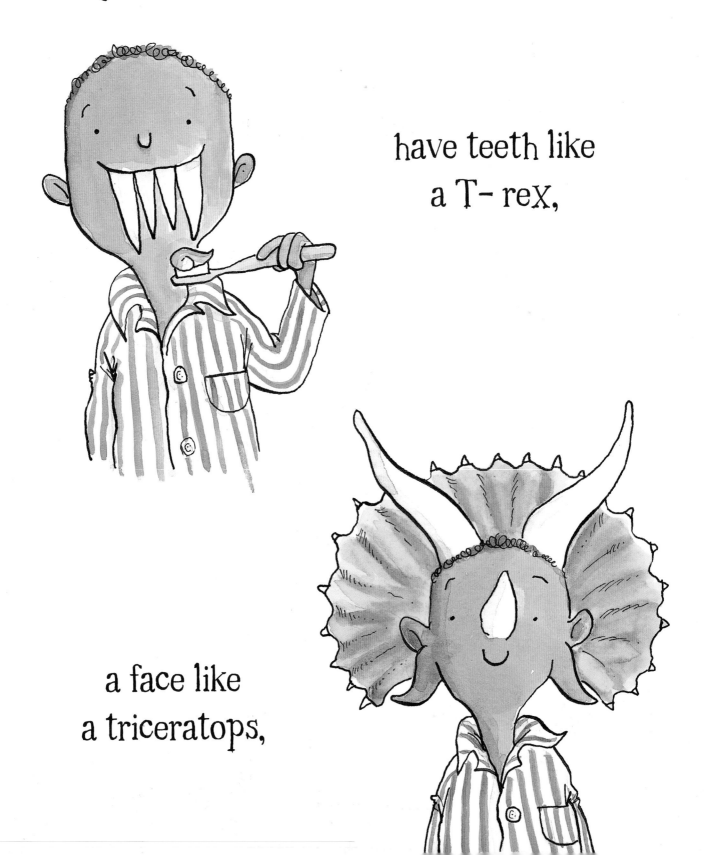

a face like
a triceratops,

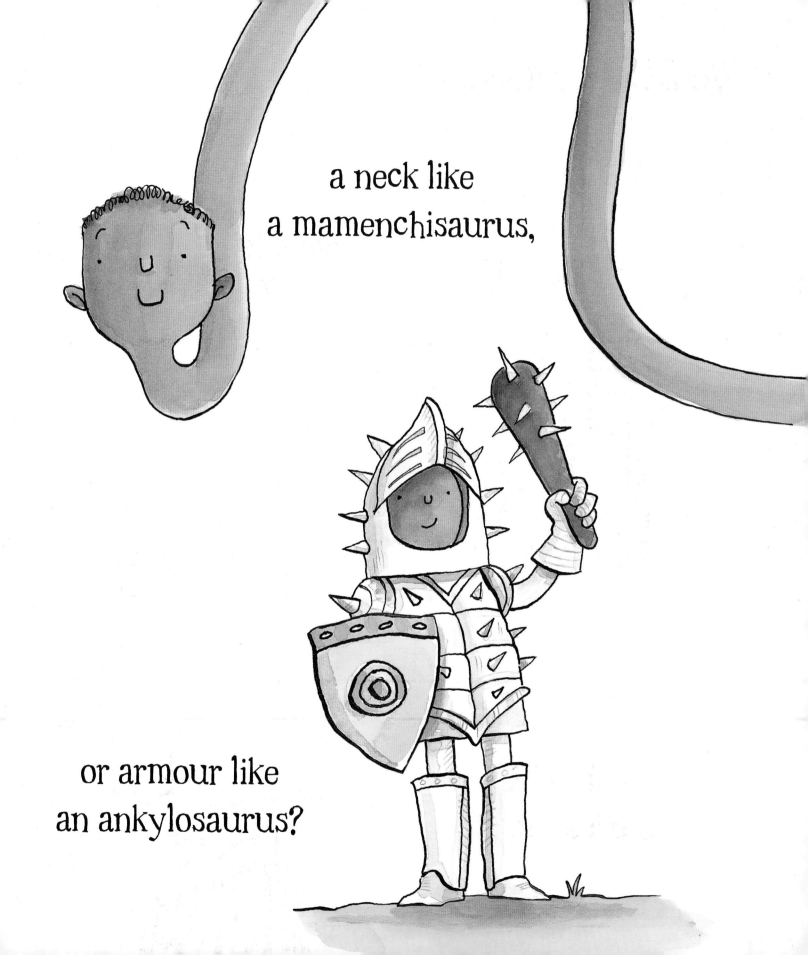

It would take ages to brush your teeth. T-rex had teeth the size of bananas!

T-rex was one of the deadliest dinosaurs that ever roamed Earth. It had huge jaws and about 60 flesh-shearing, bone-crushing teeth.

Triceratops means '3-horned face' so you'd be good at scary face competitions!

This terrifying dinosaur had a huge frill on its head. The frill may have been brightly coloured to scare other animals away.

Your neck would be as long as a bus!

A mamenchisaurus could stretch its neck to the tallest treetops and reach the juiciest leaves. A long tail helped this dinosaur keep its balance, so it didn't topple over.

You'd never win a dinosaur race but you'd be safe from predators!

An ankylosaurus had a thick armour of toughened skin, spines and spikes. It was about twice the length of an elephant but probably moved more like a tortoise because it was so big and heavy!

Would you rather go to a party with...

an edmontosaurus,

a gigantoraptor,

or a parasaurolophus?

An edmontosaurus would be great at blowing up party balloons!

It had lots of loose, baggy skin around its nose, which it could fill with air and blow up like a balloon for other dinosaurs to admire.

A gigantoraptor would spend all of its time on the dance floor looking for a tasty snack!

This dinosaur would dress to impress, looking bright, bold and beautiful – just like a bird. It was a nimble mover and could pounce to catch its prey!

A parasaurolophus would be a noisy party-pooper!

A parasaurolophus blew air through a strange crest on its head. It made ear-splitting bellowing noises that could frighten other dinosaurs away.

Would you rather live with...

an archaeopteryx,

a troodon,

Can you climb a tree? You'd have to learn if you lived with an archaeopteryx!

It was a dinosaur-like bird that could fly! It lived in trees where it was safe from other dinosaurs.

A troodon lived in the cool north so you'd need to wrap up warm!

It may have been covered in feathers to protect it from the cold. Its huge eyes helped it to find food during the long winter nights.

Don't forget your sun hat and bug spray! An ouranosaurus lived in hot, swampy places.

It had a strange 'sail' on its back, which may have helped the dinosaur to warm up in the morning, and cool down when it got too hot.

Time for a swim! A plesiosaurus was a reptile that lived in the sea at the same time as dinosaurs walked on Earth.

It had a long neck and legs that were shaped like flippers so it could swim underwater and chase tasty fish to eat.

Would you rather have...

a maiasaura
for a mum,

a diplodocus
for a dad,

an iguanodon
for a brother,

or a velociraptor
for a sister?

You'd be well looked after! This gentle dinosaur took care of her babies.

A maiasaura mum guarded her nest, protecting her brood from deadly dinosaurs. She even fetched plants to feed her young.

If you're lucky, this diplodocus dad would let you slide down his long tail.

But don't annoy him! A diplodocus could use its long tail as a whip to strike any predators that got too close.

An iguanodon would make a great brother. He'd take
good care of you and keep an eye out for danger.

Iguanodons lived
in large groups
called herds to
protect each other.
But you'd have to
be careful one
didn't step on you!

Try not to irritate your
super-smart, speedy sister!

A velociraptor was a quick-thinking and fast-moving feathered
dinosaur. It had enormous claws that it used for slashing its prey.

Would you rather have...

breakfast with a brachiosaurus,

lunch with a deinocheirus,

dinner with
a tarbosaurus,

or a snack with
a compsognathus?

Your breakfast bowl would include lots of yummy stones and leaves!

A brachiosaurus could eat up to 400 kg of plants in one day. It sometimes swallowed stones which helped to turn the tough plants into a green soupy mush that was easier to digest.

You'd need long arms to pluck your lunch from the trees!

A deinocheirus used its arms to reach into the trees to pick lots of delicious fruit. Each of its 'fingers' was longer than your arm!

Enjoy your dinner of crunchy bones with foul and rotting flesh!

A tarbosaurus hunted its prey, but it would also eat dead animals it found on the ground. This beast had a powerful bite which could crush huge bones into bite-size pieces.

You'd have to be quick to catch your snack!

A compsognathus chased bugs and fast-running lizards, which it caught with its beak-like mouth and swallowed whole.

Dinosaur Awards!

Which dinosaur would you rather be?

Ankylosaurus

The Toughest Dinosaur

The armour-plating of an ankylosaurus was so tough it would be very difficult to eat, so most other dinosaurs left the mighty beast alone.

The Heaviest Dinosaur

One of the heaviest dinosaurs to ever live was the brachiosaurus. It weighed up to 80 tonnes - that's the weight of about 16 African elephants!

Brachiosaurus

Maiasaura

The Gentlest Dinosaur

This dinosaur was gentle with its babies, and ate plants not other animals. It had lots of little teeth and horse-like hooves rather than claws.

The Scariest Dinosaur

There were bigger and faster dinosaurs, but the T-rex gets this award because it was the most fearsome of them all. It had everything: strength, speed and size!

T-rex

The Fastest Dinosaur

No one knows exactly how fast dinosaurs ran, but this little dinosaur was probably one of the fastest. If it was still alive, it would beat most humans in a running race.

Compsognathus

The Smartest Dinosaur

A troodon had a big brain and was probably one of the smartest dinosaurs around. Being smart helps an animal find food.

Troodon

More Dinosaur Fun!

Stay safe and ask a grown-up to help you.

Explore meteors

There are no dinosaurs alive today. Why not? Use books or the Internet to find out why dinosaurs became extinct (there's a clue above!). Are any modern animals in danger of becoming extinct soon? Why?

Design a dinosaur

Scientists can only guess at dinosaurs' colours and patterns. Draw your favourite dinosaur and colour it in. Look at pictures of birds, large mammals and modern reptiles, such as snakes and lizards, for ideas.

Would you rather...?

Think of some 'Would you rather...?' questions to share with your friends or family. Visit your local library and research different dinosaurs to create your own fun questions.

Footprints

Scientists find out information about dinosaurs by looking at their footprints in rock. Make a footprint trail in sand or mud, or coat the soles of your feet in paint and stamp on a large piece of paper. You will need a bowl of water to wash your feet afterwards.

Publisher: Zeta Jones
Associate Publisher: Maxime Boucknooghe
Designer: Victoria Kimonidou
Editor: Sophie Hallam
Art Director: Laura Roberts-Jensen
Editorial Director: Victoria Garrard

Copyright © QED Publishing 2016

www.quartoknows.com/brand/
2040/QED-Publishing/

First published in hardback in the UK in 2015
by QED Publishing
Part of The Quarto Group
The Old Brewery, 6 Blundell Street,
London, N7 9BH

Quarto is the authority on a wide range of topics.

Quarto educates, entertains and enriches the lives of our readers—enthusiasts and lovers of hands-on living.

www.quartoknows.com

A catalogue record for this book is available from the British Library.

ISBN 978 1 78493 200 8

Printed in China